IMAGES
of America

ITALIANS
IN CHICAGO

For Fathers
Fregonesi —
Thanks for the
Kind words
Dominic Candeloro
Columbus Day
1999

Cover Image: St. Joseph Club members and First Communion class gather with statue, banner, flags, flowers, and sashes to celebrate the (Sicilian) Feast of St. Joseph at All Saints Church in the Bridgeport neighborhood in March 1929. Somewhere in the group is Marge Sabella, who donated this photograph to the Italians in Chicago Project. (IAC 74.14.)

IMAGES
of America

ITALIANS
IN CHICAGO

Dominic Candeloro

ARCADIA

Published by Arcadia Publishing,
an imprint of Tempus Publishing, Inc.
2 Cumberland Street
Charleston, SC 29401

Printed in Great Britain.

Library of Congress Catalog Card Number: 99-63800

For all general information contact Arcadia Publishing at:
Telephone 843-853-2070
Fax 843-853-0044
E-Mail arcadia@charleston.net

For customer service and orders:
Toll-Free 1-888-313-BOOK

Visit us on the internet at http://www.arcadiaimages.com

CONTENTS

INTRODUCTION

Italians in Chicago: From Mass Migration to Ethnic Community

Italians have been a part of the Chicago community since the 1850s. Their numbers grew around the turn of the century and immigration peaked in 1914. In those early years, they were a prime source of manual labor needed in the rapidly growing city. They settled in paesani-based neighborhoods on the near north, west, and south sides of the Loop and in a half dozen industrial suburbs.

Life was not always easy for the immigrant family. Italians were often seen as objects of charity by social workers, but through it all they maintained the essential elements of their family-oriented culture. They worked hard, founded mutual benefit societies, churches, and schools, formed small family businesses, and kept their families together. Over three generations, they have moved comfortably into the middle class and into leadership positions in Chicago society. Italians have created a strong network of organizations and an ethnic community that amounts to a manageable arena for the social validation and recognition that we all crave.

Italian-American organizations have a solid place in the social pecking order of the city. The capacity of the community to maintain and promote Italian culture is enhanced by active participation from various Italian governmental agencies in the city. The population of Italian Americans in the Chicago area has experienced the classic duality of the descendants of immigrants. Though thoroughly American, to varying degrees they maintain some of the Italian family, religious, and language traditions.

This book provides approximately 200 glimpses into Chicago's Italian-American past. Each picture has a story, documented or imagined, that speaks to us of the challenge of migration, the joys, pain, and dignity of work and family life, and the pride of ethnic survival. As author of this book, I hope some readers will "see themselves in history," perhaps for the first time. I know that many will see ancestors or surrogate ancestors and begin to understand their history.

In any case, the photographs are what they are. The completeness of our sources on each photograph varies and we make no pretension that this, or any history, can be the definitive story of a large and complex group. Documenting and interpreting the history of any group is an ongoing enterprise, and I welcome dialogue with readers who have additional information and interpretations of the material covered in this volume.

–Dominic Candeloro
Chicago Heights, February 1999

ACKNOWLEDGMENTS

This photographic history has a variety of sources. About half of the images were collected as part of the National Endowment for the Humanities Italians in Chicago Project, which I directed at the University of Illinois at Chicago. I extend my warmest thanks to project staff members, especially Rose Ann Rabiola Miele, Emma Parrillo, the late Mary Ellen Mancini Batinich, Richard Della Croce, and Mary Ann Johnson for their fine work. The author gratefully acknowledges the Italian-American Collection, Special Collections Division of the University Library at the University of Illinois at Chicago, and Mary Ann Bamburger for their fine work in preserving the collection and making about 50 photographs available for this book. Photographs from this collection are identified with the "IAC" designation, and reproductions can be obtained by contacting the Special Collections Department.

Many of the photographs are part of the Italians in Chicago Exhibit (another product of the NEH grant) at the Italian Cultural Center, which is located at 1621 North 39th Avenue in Stone Park, IL, and can be contacted at (708) 345-3842. I urge interested readers to visit and support the Center.

Paul Basile, editor of the *Fra Noi* newspaper, graciously granted use of several dozen photographs that cover Italian-American organizations since the 1970s. The files of the *Fra Noi* comprise a remarkable chronicle of the Italian-American Community in Chicago since 1961. Most of the *Fra Noi* photographs were taken by Sam Bruno, the official photographer of the Italian-American community. Sam also supplied a number of celebrity and parade photographs for which I am very grateful.

The following responded to my request for family photographs and their contributions have greatly enriched and personalized the content of this book: Lisa Bacci, Nicolina Danile, Leonora LiPuma, Virginia Lizzo, Marie Pallelo, Anthony Sorrentino, Joe Tolitano, and Lucille Wrobel. Virginio Piucci helped increase the contribution of photographs. Anthony Sorrentino also assisted with the identification of many of the photographs. Space considerations made it impossible to identify all the people pictured, even when we knew who they were. We will start a file at the Italian Cultural Center. If you have additional information about a photograph, copy the photograph and send it to the Center with your expanded information about the particular photograph.

Many of the Chicago Heights photographs are available because of the hard work of the late Nick Zaranti, who collected and preserved hundreds of photographs of the city.

Readers who seek more information about the Italians in Chicago should consult Rudolph Vecoli's "Chicago's Italians Prior to World War I," (Dissertation 1961 University of Wisconsin) Humbert Nelli's, *Italians in Chicago* (Oxford 1968), my essays on "Italians in Chicago" (1995 edition), and "Chicago Heights (1984–1994 editions)" in Mel Holli and Peter

Jones (eds.) *Ethnic Chicago* (Eerdmans). These articles and others on politics and Marchegiani are or will soon be accessible on my web page, which can be reached by typing "Dominic Candeloro" at the Alta Vista search prompt.

The Italian Cultural Center Library and the Chicago Historical Society as well as the UIC IAC have transcripts of the 110 oral history interviews done as part of the Italians in Chicago Project. They are a gold mine of information for the diligent researcher.

I have had a good deal of help in preparing this book from my daughters, Anne Candeloro Klos and Gina Candeloro DeButch. Steve Modzelewski helped with proofreading. In assembling this, my second Arcadia project, I have once more relied on the organizational skills of my wife and best friend, Carol Cutlip Candeloro.

One

MIGRATION

Five million Italian immigrants came to the United States before 1914. Some of them were birds of passage, here to work a season or two, and then return to Italy. Many started on railroad jobs and were drawn to settle in their railroad's winter headquarters—Chicago. Others were attracted to Chicago by the favorable labor market in one of the fastest-growing industrial cities in the world. Chains of migration linked Chicago with towns in northern and southern Italy. Some of the towns which contributed migrants to Chicago were the following: Alta Villa Milicia, Tesche Conca, Caccamo, Lucca, Ponte Buggianese, Pievepeligo, Sant'Ana Peligo, Mola di Bari, Amaseno, San Benedetto del Tronto, Castel di Sangro, Cosenza, Pizzone, Castel San Vincenzo, and scores of others. Though we often minimize the emotional cost of emigration when we recount three-generation success stories, separations caused by emigration hurt deeply. Even the considerable financial remittances sent back to Italy by the new immigrants could not erase that pain.

These 1920s ocean passenger liners brought fewer immigrants to the United States in greater comfort than was the case in the mass immigration era before 1914.

Young paesani from the Marche region pose in Chicago Heights for this 1920s photograph. Photographs like this, implying success and contentment, were sent back to Italy and often sparked the desire of friends and family in Italy to move to America.

V. PARISE
11556 FRONT AVENUE
CHICAGO, ILL.

TENETE QUESTO CON VOI N? 8245

CHICAGO *June 10* 192*8*

RICEVUTO DAL SIG.

LA SOMMA DI LIRE

PER TRASMETTERLA AL SIG.

NELL U. P. DI

PROVINCIA DI

Lire *100.00*

The Parise Agency in Roseland helped arrange the purchase of tickets for loved ones to rejoin family members in Chicago. This receipt for a 1925 ocean liner ticket represents a momentous event in the migration saga: family reunification.

The garment worn in this photo was tailored by a father especially for his daughter's long migration trip to Chicago. He hoped that this finery would protect his daughter from the rejection and disrespect so often shown to poor immigrants. This 1890s dress is on display at the Italian Cultural Center as an artifact of the emotions surrounding the act of migration.

Chicago, Sta. 66, Ill.		39769
STAMP OF ISSUING OFFICE	Country of payment or intermediary country	AMOUNT
CHICAGO, ILL. AUG 22 1913 STA. NO. 9	*Italy* **RECEIPT** FOR INTERNATIONAL MONEY ORDER ——— REÇU d'un Mandat de Poste International Remitter should keep this receipt, which will be detached and handed to him by the issuing postmaster.	$ *20* IN FOREIGN MONEY *103 fc*

This receipt for $20 is emblematic of the millions of dollars that hard-working Chicago immigrants sent back to their families in Italy since the migration began.

The faces of the immigrants in early portraits express the dignity, purpose, and strength that allowed them to cope with and eventually thrive in their new environment. (IAC 120.6)

Two

FAMILY

For the early immigrants, family was everything. They left the family in Italy in order to save it. In Italian culture, the family is a social institution much stronger than the Church, the schools, or the government. They underconsumed and saved up money in order to create chains of migration that brought brides, mothers, cousins, and all matter of kin to join them in America. Family provides the admiring audience and the support system for life's triumphs and failures. Family gave meaning and purpose to every sacrifice and to every step up the ladder of social mobility. And family solidarity was a key reason why Italian immigrants in Chicago were able to thrive.

The baptismal party for Edward Prignano in 1932 was a very well-attended affair. The lavish celebration of baptisms, weddings, communions, confirmations, funerals, and even birthday parties kept alive family and fraternal ties and strengthened the social fabric and support system. Being part of such a family network meant never having to pay for a haircut, or home and auto repairs, or summer vegetables; it meant being able to borrow your uncle's car, and always finding a summer job. It also meant reciprocity and giving back to the family as much as you received from it. (IAC 189.16.)

Anthony and Ann Sorrentino pose at their wedding in June 1939, in front of Our Lady of Pompeii. The couple had three children and became major figures in the Joint Civic Committee of Italian Americans, the *Fra Noi*, and the Italian Cultural Center activities. Tony was a sociologist and crime-prevention youth worker and writer; Ann was famous for her cooking column and the posthumously published *Ann's Kitchen*.

Pictured is Mount Carmel Cemetery in 1943. Mary Ann (Tolitano) Cioffi, age four, and Joe Tolitano, age three, are shown kissing the stone of their grandfather's grave. Respect for family traditions and ancestors was especially pronounced in the first and second generations.

Confirmation and the godparent relationship was taken very seriously in early generations when struggling immigrants needed all the support they could muster in order to cope with the strange language, customs, and economic uncertainties. Donald Contursi and his sponsor, Peter Fosco, pose on Donald's confirmation day in the late 1930s. Fosco was a labor leader and Cook County Commissioner.

The Tarantella is captured at this 1950s wedding in Chicago Heights. After more than a century, descendants of Italian immigrants still include this "tarantella dance" on their DJ's wedding play list.

This is the Gloria and Renato Bacci wedding on June 16, 1946. The post-war era saw a rush of marriages, the formation of new families, and exodus from the central city.

This wedding reception line in the 1940s included the "busta" (envelope money gift) as well as a stiff shot of whiskey for the gentleman and anisette for the lady.

The wedding of Yolanda Giannetti and Lodovico Candeloro took place on November 29, 1931, in Chicago Heights. Weddings and families were so important that, even in the midst of the Great Depression, Italians of limited means pulled out all the stops and did everything first class. Generous money gifts from family in *buste* (envelopes) made it all possible.

This 50th wedding anniversary of Chicago Heights celebrities Giacinta (Mamma Mia) and Gaetano D'Amico took place at the Southmoor Hotel on January 17, 1935. Guests included Chicago business associates of the D'Amico Macaroni Company as well as Chicago Heights friends and relatives.

Here is a festive family celebration with the LiPuma/LaPlacas in the 1940s. The best china is on the table, the wine is ready, and the proud hostess sports a trusty print apron. (IAC 10.48.)

Three generations gather for a family birthday celebration in the late 1950s. (IAC 31.1.)

Though migration of Italians to Chicago Heights didn't start until the 1890s, by 1950 the Ricchiuto family could boast this family reunion photograph. In a family this size, opportunities for networking and exchanging services and favors were enormous and this helps to explain the strength of the support system of Italian Americans.

This Interlandi family reunion photograph in River Grove emphasizes growth over time.

Shortly after the death of Anthony Paterno, wine importer and former Joint Civic Committee president, his family and friends gathered at the Villa Scalabrini Chapel for a mass in remembrance of him. This photo was taken in December 1978.

In the 1920s, funerals were often elaborate affairs with bands, flowers, and hundreds of mourners. Mutual benefit societies were formed to help pay for these grand affairs. Photographs like this one, taken in front of St. Anthony's in Roseland, were sent as mementos to relatives in Italy.

Into the 1940s, wakes were held in the home of the deceased. This photograph of Irene Clarizio's wake in 1929 includes another custom of the day: a floral arrangement with a clock indicating the exact hour of the death. (IAC 122.5.)

In 1940, at a Tolitano family picnic held at Grass Lake, Wisconsin, the homemade wine flowed freely.

The strong Italian family tradition of piety and respect for ancestors dictated frequent family outings to Mount Carmel and other cemeteries. In this c. 1940 view, relatives tend to the Esposito/Contursi monument at Mount Carmel.

Three

WORK

Italian immigrants came to America ready and willing to work. "Pane e lavoro" (bread and work) was their goal. In comparison with conditions in the Old Country, opportunities to work in Chicago were terrific. Though a large number of the immigrants were illiterate in their own language, they possessed agrarian, handyman, and household skills that served them well in their new country. The immigrants worked hard for themselves and their families. No job was too humble and no one ever refused overtime because it ultimately helped support the family. Working conditions were horrible and industrial accidents, frequent. Many in the first and second generations literally sacrificed themselves in backbreaking jobs on construction, in the factories, and at home so that their children could have a better life.

Gaetano Bozzi is shown here with co-workers on a road repair crew. Even unskilled immigrants in the early part of the century had little trouble finding work because the economy needed them as much as the immigrants needed refuge from the problems of the old country.

Railroad workers, including Archimede Talevi, worked in Spokane, Washington, before coming to Chicago in 1906.

Railroad work, for some, offered more adventure than arduous pick-and-shovel labor. Shown here is Joe La Placa in 1912.

Railroad jobs were plentiful in the early part of the century. Joe La Placa and co-workers are shown on the Grand Trunk at Fifty-third and Kedzie.

Grand Trunk Railroad workers are shown in this 1910 scene. Many early immigrants were birds of passage here, who worked for a season or two in order to earn a nest egg and return to Italy to buy land or a business. There were railroad jobs for immigrants within the city as well as the interstate networks. Here, Italian and Polish workers on the Grand Trunk Line pose at Fifty-third Street and Kedzie Avenue in 1910. The marking beneath the third man from the left is for Gennaro Bruno.

These Montana railroad workers ended up living in Chicago, where they spent their winters. This c. 1904 photograph documents the youth of the workers, the harsh conditions of labor, and the isolation of this type of work.

Pictured is an Italian construction crew during the erection of Cook County Jail at Twenty-sixth and California Avenue in 1928. Many of the men shown here were related to one another. Standing at the extreme rear is Giacchimo Scimeca. Most belonged to the Laborers' Union, whose leadership was dominated by Italians.

Many Italian men found work on construction projects, especially in the sewer and gutter business. This crew at the county jail construction site in 1928 illustrates their camaraderie.

A major mystery and irony of immigration is that workers left San Benedetto del Tronto, a magnificent beach town on the Adriatic Sea, to come to work at the original Inland Steel Plant in Chicago Heights. This photo was taken c. 1910.

These young women worked at a pants factory in Chicago Heights in the 1940s. The friendships and family ties among the workers protected them from the harshest difficulties of the workplace.

28

By the 1940s, men with origins in the town of Ricigliano had a virtual monopoly on news-vending jobs throughout the Loop. Tradition tells us that they all sent their sons to college and law school.

Italian-American women have worked outside of the home almost since the beginning. These teens and adults worked on onion farm in South Holland. (IAC 40.14.)

Stone carvers at the Roselli Monument Company, located at Roosevelt and Wolf Roads in Hillside, prepare a piece for installation in the 1950s. Italian plaster workers, stone masons, ceramists, and terrazzo workers have contributed a great deal to the City's architecture and art.

Italian Americans were among the workers at the Pullman Company on the southern border of the city. There was also a colony of Italians who served as brick makers for the construction of Pullman. Their hard work has endured more than a century.

Four

NEIGHBORHOODS

Before 1950, Sicilians lived on the Near North Side, Riciglianesi in Chinatown, Baresi on the Near Northwest Side, Neapolitans and others resided on the Near West Side, Toscani in the Twenty-fourth and Oakley area, Marchegiani in Chicago Heights, and Modenesi in Highwood; folks from Ripacandida found homes in Blue Island. Often, it seemed, individual streets in Chicago were populated by people from the same town in Italy. In an era before the total dominance of the automobile, the neighborhood was the universe, especially for women and children. GI housing and education loans, the building of new expressways, urban-renewal projects, and the opening up of the tight post-war housing market combined to undermine the viability of the old Italian neighborhoods in Chicago. But even among those who moved to the remotest suburbs, a nostalgia for the camaraderie and sense of community in the old neighborhood continued to hold strong.

The Sorrentino family and the Peter Scalise family visit on the front steps of their home at 4320 West Adams in 1951. The city-front stoop and the small front lawn can be seen as symbols of the impending transfer of Italians from the inner city to the suburbs. Today, more than half of the 250,000 Italian ethnics in the Chicago area live outside the city limits.

Into the 1940s, it was not uncommon to see horse-drawn milk wagons and other delivery vehicles on the streets of Chicago. This young man tries out the reigns of Vito Bagnuolo's rig in the Bridgeport area.

One of the oldest continuing Italian businesses is the Gonella Bread Company depicted in this 1900 photograph. One of the highest compliments that could be paid to an Italian American was to say he was "buono come un pezzo di pane" (as good as bread).

32

The Tricarico Grocery at 1020 West Polk on a slow day in the early 1950s. In small groceries such as this, wives could tend the store and the children while husbands worked daytime jobs and returned for evening and weekend work in the store. (IAC 140.1.)

Three boys read the comics and the sports pages in front of a "Dad's Old Fashioned Root Beer" sign. This photograph conveys the attractiveness and power of nostalgia for the "old neighborhood,"an almost universal sentiment of first and second generation folks who moved to the suburbs. (IAC 178.5.)

Imported cheese and olive oil and Livingston Bread were sold at the grocery store near the home of the Puciarello family. Here they are shown in 1926 at 1101-1103 South Racine. This photograph seems to embody the essence of the pre-World War II Italian neighborhood that

engendered so much nostalgia in the generation that moved away from the central core in the 1950s and after. (IAC 135.18.)

The 1906 photograph above shows Jones School children. One of them is Roland Libonati, who later became Chicago's first Italian-American congressman in the 1950s.

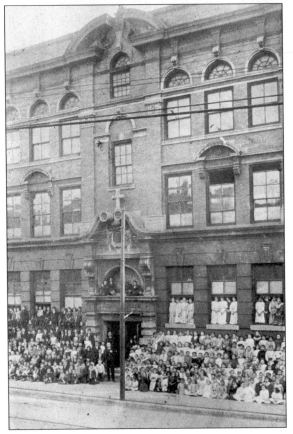

Assumption Church, now in the shadow of the Merchandise Mart, was the first Italian church in Chicago. This building, located a few blocks north, was its thriving school. The structure currently houses a photography business. This photo was taken c. 1900.

St. Philip Benizi, in the 1920s, stood at the corner of Oak and Cambridge (now Cabrini-Green), and its Servite priests led by Fr. Giambastiani ministered mainly to Sicilians in the neighborhood.

St. Philip Benizi School had a staff of 12 nuns and a very heavy enrollment of young Italian-American students in the 1940s. Within 20 years, the church and school were razed to make way for the expansion of the Cabrini-Green Housing Project. (IAC 91.12.)

The graduation class from Riis School on the Near West Side is shown here in 1930. More than 90% of those pictured are Italian American.

Italian-American veterans march in Roseland in the 1930s. Service in the military was a major step toward Americanization. (IAC 55.69.3.)

More than half of this All Saints (St. Anthony) School (Bridgeport) eighth-grade class were of Italian origin. The schools were a major Americanizing force.

The Rosary Society of Saint Anthony of Padua Church in Roseland is shown here in a 1950s street procession.

Nardi men carefully tend the backyard garden of their Bridgeport home at 2809 South Wells in 1968. Resourceful Italian immigrants used large gardens for economic, spiritual, and gastronomical purposes. It is only a small exaggeration to say that many Italian Americans moved into the middle class on the basis of two generations of expansive gardening. (IAC 103.8.)

Villa residents show the fruit of their hunt for ciccoria in the 1970s. In springtime, these greens are abundant in lawns and fields. Resourceful Italian immigrants and their descendants, no matter how poor, always had access to this nutritious dandelion-type "weed," which was prepared as a salad or boiled and fried in olive oil and garlic.

Paesani from Scaroni (Potenza), enjoying the day in the backyard on the West Side, are (from left to right) Sam Pernetti, Dominic DiMucci, and Saverio Dallesandro.

Residents of the Villa competed for high ratings on home-grown tomatoes. Gardening for the first few generations of Italian immigrants made an economic, psychological, and dietary contribution to family and neighborhood life. This photo was taken in 1975.

Renato Capecci, Aunt Gemma Novelli, and Julio Narcisi, who later became fire chief, are shown in front of an East Side corner store, Novelli's Grocery in Chicago Heights, in the 1930s. In the old neighborhoods, commerce and shopping had a personal and familiar dimension.

Chicago Heights friends of the second generation address their bocce toss to the camera in the 1930s. (IAC 188.9.)

Five

RELIGION

Italian immigrants came to America with their own brand of Catholicism, which sometimes clashed with the established Irish-oriented hierarchy. Anti-clericalism among political radicals, also undermined the faith. The building of a dozen churches and schools by the Scalabrini order gave direction and leadership to the Italian communities by 1925. Protestants, anarchists, and others tried to bring "lax" Italian Catholics to their ranks with only minimal success. In the end, the Scalabrini Fathers overcame obstacles and melded Italian culture with the Catholic faith. The final product for Italian Americans after three generations was integration into a shared Chicago ethnic Catholicism. By the end of the 20th century, many of the Italian Catholic institutions had served their purpose and faced declining support.

Mother Cabrini, the Italian-American saint, died in Chicago in 1916 after founding schools, nurseries, and a hospital.

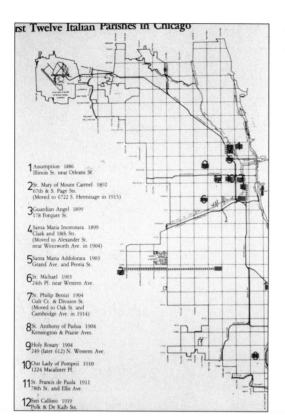

1 Assumption 1886
Illinois St. near Orleans St.

2 St. Mary of Mount Carmel 1892
67th & S. Page Sts.
(Moved to 6722 S. Hermitage in 1915)

3 Guardian Angel 1899
178 Forquer St.

4 Santa Maria Incoronata 1899
Clark and 18th Sts.
(Moved to Alexander St.
near Wentworth Ave. in 1904)

5 Santa Maria Addolorata 1903
Grand Ave. and Peoria St.

6 St. Michael 1903
24th Pl. near Western Ave.

7 St. Philip Benizi 1904
Galt Ct. & Division St.
(Moved to Oak St. and
Cambridge Ave. in 1914)

8 St. Anthony of Padua 1904
Kensington & Prairie Aves.

9 Holy Rosary 1904
249 (later 612) N. Western Ave.

10 Our Lady of Pompeii 1910
1224 Macalister Pl.

11 St. Francis de Paula 1911
78th St. and Ellis Ave.

12 San Callisto 1919
Polk & De Kalb Sts.

This map shows the major Italian Catholic churches in Chicago. The vast majority of them were staffed by Scalabrini Fathers.

Since the early part of the century, Scalabrini priests organized their countrymen to build churches and schools in a dozen Chicago parishes. Northerners from the Piacenza area, they often felt overwhelmed and out of place ministering to southern-Italian peasant immigrants, but they persevered and triumphed. This photograph was taken in the 1920s.

This late-1930s photograph shows Sacred Heart seminarians and their teachers at Santa Maria Addolorata on the Near Northwest Side. The seminary, which moved to the building in Stone Park that is now the Italian Cultural Center, was meant to produce American-born Scalabrini priests to minister to the Italian-American community.

Periodically, the Scalabrini priests in the province of St. John (Ohio and West, including some of Canada) meet in Chicago to discuss new policies, personnel transfers, and other matters. There are about 500 Scalabrinians throughout the world dedicated to serving immigrants, Italian and otherwise. As the status and the numbers of Italian immigrants change, so does the role of this order of priests.

In June 1978, St. Michael in the Twenty-fourth and Oakley neighborhood celebrated its 75th anniversary. This is especially notable because anti-clerical Tuscan socialists and anarchists gave active resistance to the Scalabrini priests who organized the parish in the early decades of the century.

Fr. Pacifico, at San Rocco in Chicago Heights, celebrated his Silver Jubilee mass in 1938.

First Communion class poses in May 1956 at St. Anthony of Padua in Roseland. The arrangements of saints on the altar was typical of Catholic church design in that era. (IAC 106.4.)

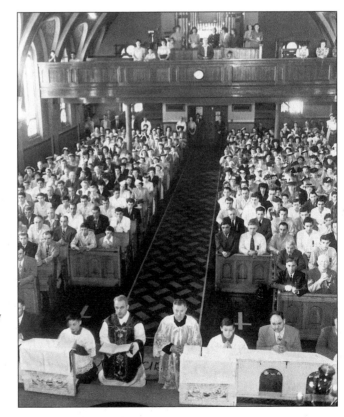

This 1950s mass at St. Anthony of Padua was apparently related to a men's society. Note the society ribbons and the fact that the first six rows are occupied by men. (IAC 55.23.4.)

Parishioners gather with Papal, Italian, and American flags and society banners to celebrate the Concordat between Mussolini and the Pope on June 29, 1929, at our Lady of Pompeii Church.

The Feast of St. Philip Benizi, April 14, 1929, depicts a parish at the height of its glory with thousands of parishioners and dozens of sodalities and societies. Most outsiders (including

FESTA DELLA CONCILIAZIONE
FRA LA CHIESA E LO STATO IN ITALIA
CELEBRATA DALLA PARROCCHIA DELLA MADONNA DI POMPEI
IL GIORNO 9 DI GIUGNO 1929

The agreement ended a half century of strife between church and state in Italy.

sociologist Harvey Zorbaugh) probably considered this Near North Side Sicilian neighborhood a dangerous slum. (IAC 186.1.)

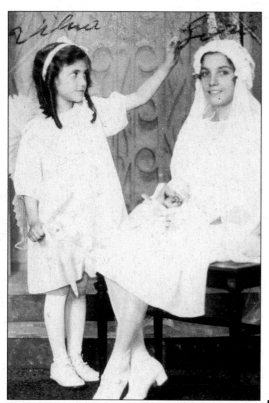

"Angels" usually led processions at First Communion and Confirmation events. Catholic schools and Catechism classes connected ethnic children with the Chicago Catholic culture, which speeded Americanization and acceptance in this city. This photo was taken c. 1935.

First Communion was an important event. It was a religious occasion that called for an enormous extended family party and gifts. These two young girls were photographed c. 1918.

This First Communion photograph of girls on on the front stoop is unusual in that it features a dog.

In this 1974 view, the faithful pray the steps of the Calvary Hill, on the grounds of the Sacred Heart Seminary (now the Italian Cultural Center and Casa Italia), in Stone Park.

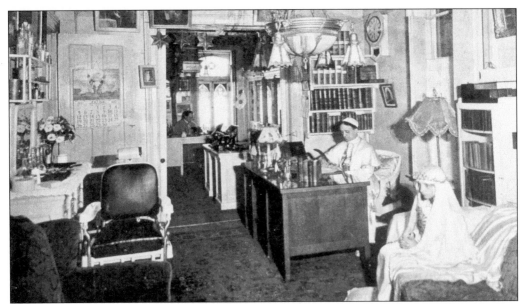

A renegade former barber, Giuseppe Abate organized a crypto Catholic church of his own on the Near West Side. The "Celestial Messenger," as he called himself, dressed in papal fashion and posed in his office with a young girl identified as the "Virgin Mary at age 12" on the couch in 1919. Note the barber chair "relic."

The old Our Lady of Mount Carmel church structure is shown in Melrose Park under demolition in the 1960s.

Shown in the 1930s, Rev. Pasquale De Carlo works with Joseph Tuzzolino at the St. John Institutional Church Vacation Bible School. He is putting the finishing touches on a model village created by the young people as part of the city's summer program to keep youth off the streets.

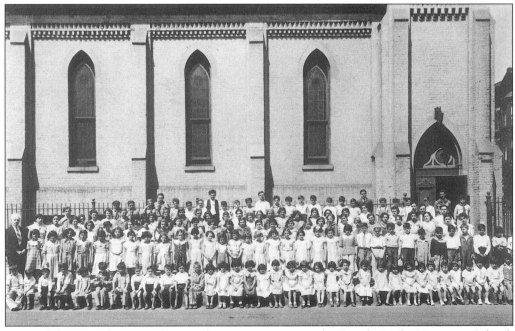

Pictured here is the St. John Presbyterian Institutional Church Daily Vacation School. (IAC 19930s.)

The Italian Catholic Federation attracted participation from a large number of local and West Coast adherents at its national conferences in the 1970s and 1980s.

Sister Agnes Campisi was inducted into the City of Chicago Senior Citizen Hall of Fame in 1976. A member of the Missionary Sisters of the Sacred Heart, she was personally inducted into the Order in 1901 by Chicago's Saint, Mother Cabrini.

Six
BUSINESS AND THE PROFESSIONS

Chicago's Italian Americans have achieved at the highest levels in business and in other professions. The earliest advances involved humble grocery stores, barbershops, bars, shoe repair shops, and small restaurants. Italians have been blessed with a popular cuisine, and have translated that advantage into thousands of successful family restaurants and other food-related businesses. By the third generation, Italian names have become well-represented in the medical and legal professions and in the business world. Leaders in Law, Medicine, Sports, and Religion, as well as major grocery chains and high-profile restaurants and auto dealerships, are all evidence of the remarkable achievements of Italian Americans in Chicago.

The Coco Grocery Store on the South Side sold fresh spring chickens in the late 1930s. Slaughtering chickens at home required skill and agility. By-products of the chicken included feather-filled pillows, blood pudding, chicken brains, and chicken feet.

Proud proprietors stand in front of their stock of fresh meat. Italian Americans have been prominent in Chicago in small family businesses since the 1920s. Food stores and meat markets provided regional specialties to customers in the reconstituted villages that became Italian neighborhoods. Note the sawdust on the floor.

The Italian American Cooperative of Chicago Heights was led by Umberto Lisciani and Alexander Lauteri and consisted of a co-op store, offices, and a banquet hall. Early published reports claimed it as part of the socialist movement. This view is from 1909.

This 1910 photograph depicts an Italian grocery store. Note the standards of display and merchandising in the early corner stores. Though the sign says that the only terms were cash, most small groceries allowed credit, and grocers were often ruined during the Great Depression when out-of-work customers defaulted.

The business lunch was 25¢, steak 35¢, and frosty beer was probably 10¢ at this typical bar in the 1930s.

Oxydal, Lava Soap, and Carnation Condensed Milk were among the icons of radio commercials in the 1930s and 1940s. Such items were available in stores like the one above.

Maria Marchetti's grocery store was located on the Near West Side. It is shown here in 1915.

The Near West Side was the location of Leo and Giovanni Marchetti's saloon, which is depicted in this 1918 photograph.

With a small storefront, a few hundred dollars worth of belt-driven machinery, and little bit of training, a factory or construction worker could become a small businessman in the shoe-repair business. The Gaylords' "Italian Shoemaker" hit of the 1950s epitomized this profession.

From left to right are Mario, Mario, Mario, Mario, Mario, etc. In the early 1980s, Mario Avignone invented Mario Day (March 10), and invited all people who shared his name to a gala dinner in support of the Villa Scalabrini. Avignone's "Pedals from Roseland" column in the *Fra Noi* has for the past 30 years been a fascinating chronicle of the Italians in that neighborhood.

The Chesrow Drugstore on the northwest corner of Taylor and Halsted in the 1950s was one of several operated by Frank Chesrow. A pharmacist from a high-achieving Calabrian family, Chesrow (Ceasario) had a distinguished career in the U.S. military and became a Cook County commissioner. Chesrow was also an avid collector of art. (IAC 213.29.)

A Taylor Street tradition is Chiaruggi's hardware, which has supplied Italian ethnics with presses, grinders, and other wine-making essentials for many generations.

Mancinelli family members are shown in front of their Near West Side watch repair and jewelry shop in 1911. This photograph provides strong evidence of a class of small business owners early in the century.

This Claudio Pastry photograph evokes the artistry, pride, and attention to detail that Italian-American small businessmen and artisans brought to their craft. Since weddings were considered so important and cost was often no object, the floral, catering, dressmaking, tuxedo rental, and pastry businesses flourished among Italian Americans. (IAC 226.7.)

D'Amato's Grocery in the heart of Bridgeport was typical of family businesses that had adjoining living quarters. The girl in the white apron is Rose Ann Rabiola Miele.

Joe Tolitano parlayed a chain of shoe repair shops into U.S. Shoe Repair with prominent downtown locations and, in 1981, opened the Institute for Shoe Repair. Tolitano was also active in this era as president of the Joint Civic Committee of Italian Americans.

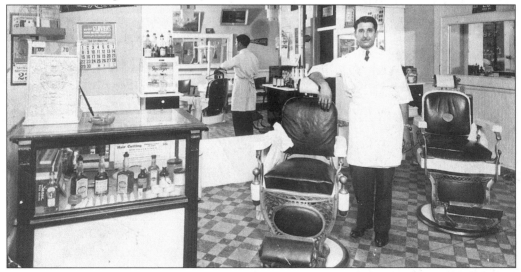

"At your service!" Tom Scalia represents a generation of Italian-American men who moved up from working class to small business as neighborhood barbers. The shop was located at 438 West Thirty-first Street in the 1940s. Into the 1960s, the Barbers' Union was mostly Italian American. (IAC 106.3.)

Gloria Talevi Bacci is shown in front of Mary Corlandesi's store (Gladys & California), in 1943. At corner stores like this one, neighbors exchanged gossip, news of the boys at the front, and family developments.

In 1981, the Calderone brothers celebrated the 50th anniversary of their Palermo restaurant (located at Sixty-third and Hamlin) with the visit of a beautiful blond actress. The restaurant is famous for the lavish St. Joseph Day charity feast, which it sponsors each year.

Amabile Santacaterina (right) is in the kitchen of the Belvidere, her restaurant at Grand Avenue and Austin Boulevard in 1950. Her legacy was passed on in the form of frozen-pasta products under the Mrs. Belgo brand name, owned by the Romanucci Company.

This photograph shows the interior of the famous Como Inn that has been operated by the Marchetti family since the 1920s. The popularity of Italian cuisine has created great opportunities for Italian-American economic advancement.

The Roselli Brothers' shop is situated in Hillside, near the major cemeteries.

The Damiani (Marchigiani) family found success in the house moving business in the 1920s in Chicago Heights. The skill and resourcefulness demonstrated in this photograph is impressive.

Joe Pagoria's Garage (family origin Caccamo, Sicily) on Lincoln Highway in the 1920s benefited from the growth of traffic on the transcontinental highway. In Chicago Heights, Sicilian immigrants, from the beginning, showed a strong inclination to get involved in small business.

Employees of the company that installed the terrazzo mosaic esplanade pose for a photograph near the Planetarium on June 20, 1933, at the Century of Progress Fair.

Italian Americans are well represented in the legal profession. The Justinian Society of Lawyers has roots that go back to the beginning of the century. Distinguished Chicago judges of Italian origin include Anthony Scariano and Nicholas Bua. Justinians admitted to the bar of the U.S.

Supreme Court posed for this 1960s photograph on the steps of the Supreme Court with Congressman Roland Libonati.

Joseph C. Mullen (left) presents an award to one of the top achievers in the Italian-American community, Federal Judge Nicholas Bua, who rendered many historic decisions, including one that curtailed patronage hiring in Cook County.

Band leader/vocalist Paul Ciminello congratulates the legendary Joe Petrillo, longtime leader of the Musicians' Union in Chicago in this early 1980s photograph. Petrillo fought hard for the royalty rights of live musicians facing the challenges of the recording industry. The band shell in Grant Park is named after Petrillo.

The Highwood Fire Department is shown in this c. 1920 photograph. The descendants of Modenese ancestors, Highwood Italians have a reputation for being more fluent in Italian than any other Chicago-area community.

Seven
BALBO'S FLIGHT

The Chicago newspapers in the 1930s rarely had a good word to say about Italians until Italo Balbo came on the scene with his transatlantic squadron. The pioneer aviator guided his squadron of 24 seaplanes from Italy to Chicago in a grand gesture that captured the imagination of the American public. Tradition has it that every Italian in town who could possibly get away went down to the Century of Progress Fair to greet Balbo and celebrate. Who could blame them for basking in the reflected glory of this dashing hero. At last, respect for something Italian!

Balbo and his men gathered at the entrance of the Italian Pavilion at the Century of Progress Fair in July 1933. Consul General Giuseppe Castruccio had labored mightily to achieve this public relations triumph for Fascist Italy.

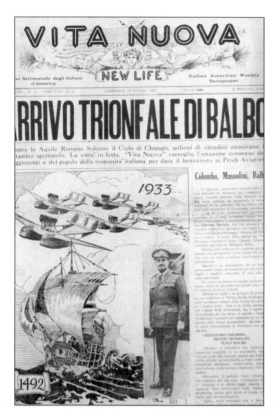

The arrival of Italo Balbo and his transatlantic flying squadron of 24 seaplanes at the Century of Progress Fair July 15, 1933, was the single proudest moment in Chicago's Italian-American history.

To aid Balbo at the dais, 21-year-old Gus Lazzerini (left of microphone) stepped forward to translate as Balbo urged Chicago Italian Americans to be proud Americans, but never forget that they are also Italians. This duality was a serious challenge to the second generation, especially when World War II broke out.

THEY CAME—THEY SAW—THEY CONQUERED

CARRY AMERICAN HEARTS AWAY.—The bronzed sons of Italy who fly the airplanes under command of Gen. Italo Balbo carried with them the affection of all Chicago when they began their homeward journey after crossing the Atlantic to the world's fair. In the photo at top, the military party is welcomed at the Italian pavilion at the fair; below, the victorious flyers move in autos along the Avenue of Flags

TIMES Photos by Max Kolin)

Thousands of Italians were in the crowd that welcomed Balbo and 100 crew men. It was easily the proudest moment of the 20th century for Chicago's Italians.

In honor of Balbo's transatlantic flight, the city of Chicago renamed Eighth Street after him. In August 1968, the corner of Michigan and Balbo was the scene of an anti-Vietnam War disturbance during the Democratic Convention. African-American activists who see Balbo as a villain for the role he played in Italy's African campaign have attempted several times to change the name of the street, but so far "Balbo" lives on.

Gilda Dentino and a friend pose in front of the Italian Pavilion at the Century of Progress Fair in 1933. The Italian-American self image over time has been closely linked with public esteem or lack thereof for the nation of Italy. Balbo and the fair gave Italians a big boost. (IAC 198.17.)

The Sunday July 23, 1933 *Times* rotogravure section paid tribute to the departure of the gallant Italo Balbo. The avalanche of positive press that accompanied the Balbo flight was in stark contrast to the steady stream of gangster news stories that besmirched the image of Italian Americans in the city of Al Capone.

Balbo unveils the Grant Park Columbus statue (near Columbus Drive and Twelfth Street) during his brief 1933 visit. Note the motto on the base: "This monument has seen the glory of the wings of Italy led by Italo Balbo. . ." Fifty years later, the monument stood witness to a series of Feste Italiane, which took place on the field north of the statue.

Italian-American club leaders gather in the 1980s with a delegation of the original Balbo crew in front of the Roman Column monument that was given by Mussolini to Chicago commemorate the one-year anniversary of the flight. It stands east of Soldier Field, near the boat harbor.

Eight

FESTE!

The survival of colorful street processions of saints is one of the most surprising aspects of Italian-American culture. Though some of the details have changed, the Mount Carmel Feast in Melrose Park is going strong after more than 100 years! Feste afford entertainment for all ages. Family tradition, paesani practices, religious faith, and sometimes, economic motives have combined to support at least 30 major and minor feasts in the Chicago area. For some feste, the venue has changed from neighborhood streets to a shopping center parking lot in the case of Santissima Maria Lauretana and in the case of San Francesco Di Paola, the Italian Cultural Center.

Shown here is Our Lady of Mount Carmel at the 50th Anniversary Feast, which was held at Melrose Park in 1944. Prayers to end World War II were preeminent among the faithful. Elaborate light displays are common in both Italy and America. (IAC 87.21.)

Though religion is usually the main responsibility of the females in the Italian-American family, males in all manner of ecclesiastical dress dominate the area nearest the Madonna. Shown here is a 1980s view of this Catholic tradition in Melrose Park.

Women bear the heavy burden of the St. Joseph "candle house" as part of the tribute to Our Lady of Mount Carmel in Melrose Park in this 1980s view. Elaborate and unique, the candle house candles are rarely lighted. Many observers felt that street processions with statues of saints would be among the first Italian traditions to fall by the wayside in the Protestant and Irish-Catholic American environment.

LA GRANDE FESTA DELLA
Madonna Del Carmine
SOLENNEMENTE
Si Celebrera' A Melrose Park
IL 16 LUGLIO 1933
PRECEDUTA DA CINQUE GIORNI DI FESTA CIOE' 11, 12, 13, 14, 15 LUGLIO

AVVISO

Chi intende di avere l' onore di portare la Statua della Madonna dovra' fare l' offerta in tempo, prima che cominci la processione, dovendo essere vestiti in divisa: e non potranno essere cambiati durante la processione stessa.

Per il buon andamento della Festa e necessaria l' unione e la concordia fra il comitato e il popolo. Nessuno potra' fare collete per fuochi ed altro senza l' authorizzazione del Parroco in scritto.

Candele o torcie si possono avere alla porta della Chiesa.

++

The Feast of
Our Lady of
Mt. Carmel

WILL BE CELEBRATED AT

Melrose Park, Sunday, July 16

PRECEDED BY FIVE DAYS OF FESTIVITIES, JULY 11, 12, 13, 14 AND 15

++

COMITATO ONORARIO
La Societa' Delle Signore Italiane di Maria SS. Del Carmine, La Congrega Di Maria Vergine Del Carmine

HONORARY PRESIDENTS OF FEAST
JOHN ROSSI   PAUL RAGO

THE CHURCH COMMITTEE

JOSEPH RAUZI   FRANK MONTINO   PELLEGRINO MOCCIA
                                President JOHN ROSSI

This 1933 flyer for the Melrose Park feast of Our Lady of Mount Carmel is bilingual. It dutifully lists committee members and the rules for those who wish to have the honor of carrying the statue. There is also a warning to beware of unauthorized solicitations for the charity.

August Feast of San Donatus in Blue Island illustrates the practice of attaching cash contributions to the statue. Many of the Italian Americans in Blue Island trace their origins to Ripacandida in the Basilicata Region. The Bishop-Saint apparently had a pretty good day. (IAC 87.57.)

The Society of San Rocco di Potenza, shown here in its procession from the Holy Rosary Church in 1979, is an example of the dramatic religious traditions that continue the ethnic identity of Italian Americans.

Strocchia concert band, photographed here in 1925, was an institution in the Italian community for many years, playing at feasts, parades, funerals, and concerts. (IAC 205.5)

The Feast of Santo Crocifisso is celebrated by immigrants from the town of Rutigliano. This photograph, taken early in the century, is from the Near North Side.

In this 1940s view, ladies dress up and wear corsages in honor of the (Sicilian) Santo Crocifisso observance at St. Philip Benizi. (IAC 186.29.)

Chinatown residents with origins in Ricigliano (Basilicata) bear the statue of Santa Maria Incoronata (meaning "crowned") through their neighborhood in the late 1950s. The striking similarity between this image and that of the same event in their Italian town of origin is convincing evidence of cultural retention. (IAC 58.15.)

Shown here is the St. Joseph of Bagheria Festival along Cambridge Street. It was held near St. Philip Benizzi in the 1930s, on the Near North Side. In that era, it is said that there was a Sicilian patron saints' feast just about every Sunday in the summer. (IAC 91.178.)

Fr. Peter Gandolfi celebrates a mass in honor of Saint John Bosco at the Italian Cultural Center pavilion in the mid-1980s.

The third annual Grape Festival Dinner took place on September 12, 1942, at the CYO Center, at 1145 West Vernon Park. Italian-American youth in the first half of this century were often the object of anti-delinquency and other social service efforts. Anthony Inorio, a protegé of Bishop Bernard Shield, was the director of this group. (IAC 144.2.)

This is a March 1974 suburban attempt to create a new tradition for the St. Joseph Feast featuring a "live saint." Knights of Columbus stand at attention. The event got off to a wobbly start. Most subsequent celebrations of St. Joseph's Day have contented themselves with elaborate meatless food tables.

The Sicilian Band of Chicago, led by Maestro Franco Albian, is one of the few large surviving Italian bands left in the nation. They appear at larger feste and at Milwaukee's Festa Italiana. (1980s.)

Unico's Festa Italiana, in the early 1990s, was held at Jacob Arvey Field in Grant Park. Four generations after immigration, the peddler's cart was still in evidence—this time more for fun and profit than for survival.

This is opening day at Festa Italiana, at Navy Pier in August 1981. Unico President Anthony Fornelli spearheaded the annual Lakefront "Celebration of Italian-American Life " into the 1990s. Attendance was 100,000 that year, and proceeds were used to support Italian-American cultural and charitable causes.

Nine
SOCIAL ORGANIZATIONS

There are hundreds of Italian-American organizations in Chicago. The author apologizes in advance for being unable to include them all. These groups have supported immigrants, provided opportunities for underprivileged kids, maintained relations with Italian towns of origin, awarded scholarships, and provided ethnic/professional support. In addition to their good works, the organizations have created an opportunity for recognition and honor both within and beyond the Italian-American community for their leaders and members. The continued vitality of Italian-American clubs and organizations is a major element in the retention of Italian ethnicity in Chicago.

This photograph of heroes killed in World War I from the northern Italian town of Treppo Grande was an icon in the home of immigrants who were not quick to forget the people and the struggles of their home town.

Though most Chicago Italians were from central or southern Italy, several notable colonies from northern Italy settled in Chicago neighborhoods. This group, probably based in the Roseland-Pullman area, hailed from Lago di Garda. Toscani from Ponte Buggianese and Lucca settled in the Twenty-fourth and Oakley area, migrants from Altopiano Asiago in Roseland, and Modena in Highwood.

Early mutual-benefit societies based on town of origin provided health and death benefits as well as fellowship for the paesani. Pictured here are the men of the Chiuppanese Society on June 8, 1913, in Kensington, adjacent to Roseland. (IAC 69.346.)

The Circolo Vicentinese from Roseland gathered for this 1925 photograph. Though most Chicago Italians had southern origins, many Roseland Italians hailed from the area around the Altopiano Asiago. (IAC 120.9.)

Organizations such as church sodalities and mutual benefit organization based on home town ties, helped the immigrant community. This group was photographed c. 1935.

Soldatini (little soldiers) at Santa Maria Incornata Church were undoubtedly inspired by the popularity of Il Duce. The flags, fasces, and the images of dignitaries in the background of this 1930s photo illustrate the coexisting American and Italian loyalties that became disrupted when the United States entered WW II.

One can only imagine the high spirits of *le donne* (women) dancing in the Cook County Forest Preserve. This event took place in the 1930s.

The Highwood Chamber of Commerce banquet was held January 25, 1932, at the St. James Hall. Many business leaders of this town were immigrants and sons of immigrants from the Modenese towns of Pieve Peligo and Sant' Ana Peligo. Consult Adria Bernardi's *Houses With Names* for more information on Highwood Italians.

The Italian Women's Prosperity Club in Highwood was one of the most important organizing forces among the Italians in that community. This event appears to be a Mardi Gras party in the 1950s. Consult Gloria Nardini's *Che Bella Figura!* for more information on this group. (IAC 132.2.)

St. Anthony Sodality of Kensington forms a procession for the feast of their patron saint in Roseland during June in the late 1930s. (IAC 55.22.1.)

In the 1940s, under the leadership of Joseph Salerno, the Italian Welfare Council sponsored the Jolly Boys and Girls Camp. The retreat was a 25-room structure set on seven acres on Pistake Bay, Wisconsin, which allowed deserving Italian inner-city kids to experience the joys of outdoor life.

This sort of banquet became typical of fund-raising events in the 1950s as Italian Americans sought to fund the Villa Scalabrini, the St. Charles Seminary, and other projects.

This is a photograph of a typical 1940s banquet of the Lucatorto family. Probably over 90% of the fund-raisers in the Italian-American community involved dinners of one sort or another.

The Societies of Our Lady of Pompeii Church held an annual dinner dance at a downtown hotel in the 1950s. Even in the 1990s, on any given Saturday night from September to May there is an Italian-American dinner dance going on at a banquet hall or downtown hotel somewhere in the Chicago area. (IAC 14.1.)

Mazzini-Verdi Ladies Auxiliary Club staged an international feast in the summer of 1982. The club rooms of the Mazzini-Verdi group feature indoor, carpeted bocce courts.

Lucchesi Nel Mondo Society is seen here at an international congress in December 1982. The Lucchesi in Chicago began as makers of plaster statues and eventually became the most business-oriented Chicago paesani group engaged in the importation of olive oil, wine, and other products.

At group meetings like this one in the basement of Our Lady of Pompeii Church, Near West Side residents organized in the 1950s in order to to redevelop their neighborhood. They were severely disappointed when the Richard J. Daley Administration determined to build the University of Illinois at Harrison and Halsted, displacing more than half of the residents. The legendary Florence Scala emerged as the leader of the fruitless effort to save the neighborhood. (IAC 189.14.)

Members of the San Bucca (Sicily) Society gathered at the Jack Nicolosi home in the fall of 1979 to celebrate the feast of the Madonna della San Bucca. The strength of hometown ties for the paesani has continued for over a century.

Members of the Tuscan Club meet at the Maroons (soccer) Club with a delegation from the Tuscany Region in an example of the countless exchanges that continue and enrich the sense of regional identity into the third and fourth generations.

Members of the Italo American National Union pose after presenting Lou Salvino with the *Culo de Cavallo* Award in 1985. It was all in good fun and for a charitable cause.

The men of the Italian American Executives of Transportation gather for a dinner in honor of Fr. Pierini's birthday in the early 1980s. Pierini was successful at getting almost every Italian American organization to consider the Villa among their favorite charities and to compete with each other in their generosity to the cause.

While many pass on traditions through churches, clubs, and organizations, others transmit cultural skills and values within the home. A father and son from the third-generation Lizzo family are shown here making wine.

Order Sons of Italy celebrate a special day at Villa Scalabrini in this July 1978 photograph. OSIA is one of the oldest and most widespread of all Italian-American organizations.

Since the late 1970s, the Italian Cultural Center has sponsored a Carnevale Dinner Dance that attracts up to 1,000 guests. Dinner proceeds, plus the profits from the ample ad-book, support the Italian Cultural Center. Perennial chairs, Leonora LiPuma and Joe Bruno, pose above the proud committee members in this late 1980s view.

Norwood Park Unico group sponsored a skating party for these young people. Unico is an Italian-American service club similar to the Kiwanis.

During Christmas in the 1980s, Villa Scalabrini residents demonstrate their appreciation for sizable donations from the major Italian-American organizations and clubs.

Josephine and Rose Ortale have been stalwart workers for the Joint Civic Committee, the Villa Scalabrini, and the Gregorian Society (of Educators). In the early 1980s, they were honored by the *Fra Noi* for a sizable memorial gift to the Villa.

Ten
VILLA SCALABRINI

The Villa Scalabrini Home for the Aged in Northlake was the brainchild of Fr. Armando Pierini. In the post WW II era, Pierini persuaded Italian Americans to adopt this as their major city-wide project. Since then, the establishment, expansion, and maintenance of the Villa have been the prime motivators that brought Italian Americans together in a powerful coalition to create this $12,000,000 institution. Though administrative changes in the 1990s diminished the Italian focus of the Villa, promotion of the Villa remains a significant element in the community, and Italian Americans still take great pride in the institution.

This is an early (1948) cartoon drawing of Villa Scalabrini, which was an appeal and a visionary mission statement by Fr. Armando Pierini. It all came true.

Old and bereft of funds, sick and incapable of working, neglected and deserted, many Italians approach the sunset of their lives with fear, uncertainty and, in some instances, despair. The plight of these aged Italians brings us face to face with problems

In the late 1940s and early 1950s, the principal means of supporting the Villa Scalabrini was the annual Italian Fair held in the Cicero Berwyn area. This aerial view of the grounds explains the magnitude of the two-week event, which required some 500 volunteers each night to staff the concessions. Joe De Serto was the perennial chair of the gargantuan event.

Fr. Armando Pierini, the most accomplished leader in the Italian community, welcomes Italian Consul General Medrine and his family to the Villa Scalabrini Home for the Aged. In the background is a bust of Scalabrini, the bishop who founded the religious order dedicated to serving Italian immigrants.

The audience at a Villa Scalabrini mortgage burning in the Auditorium Theater was treated to a performance featuring Frank Sinatra, Tony Bennett, and Fr. Armando Pierini in the 1970s.

Fr. Paul Asciolla, Frank Sinatra, Frank Annunzio, and Tony Bennett are backstage at the Mortgage Burning Gala in the 1970s.

"The dream of the Italian people of metropolitan Chicago has come true"

COME AND SEE

SOLEMN DEDICATION OF

VILLA SCALABRINI

=The Italian Old Peoples Home=

HIS EMINENCE

Cardinal Samuel A. Stritch

Officiating

On SUNDAY, JULY 1st 1951

Wolf Road, two blocks north of North Avenue
Melrose Park, Illinois

PROGRAM:

12:15 P. M. Solemn High Mass—Outdoors.
1:00 to 3:30 P. M. Refreshments, Games and Entertainment.
4:00 P. M. Blessing new Edifice by His Eminence Cardinal Samuel A. Stritch.

Participation of religious and civil dignitaries, Church Societies and civic organizations.   Music by the Italian Festival Choral Group.

TRANSPORTATION:

Westchester elevated to 25th Avenue, Bellwood. Taxicab to and from "Villa Scalabrini".

Lake Street elevated to Marion Street, Oak Park. Lake Street Bus to 25th Avenue, Melrose Park. Taxicab to and from "Villa Scalabrini".

North Avenue or Grand Avenue to Wolf Road by Automoble (Between North and Grand Avenues on Wolf Road)

Italian Parishes will arrange BUS TRANSPORTATION from CHURCH to "VILLA SCALABRINI.

Every person of Italian descent should be present at the dedication.   488

Here is the proud announcement of the opening of the Villa Scalabrini, which for more than 40 years was the main object of Italian-American philanthropy in the Chicago area.

Here is an early fund-raiser for the Villa at the Stevens (now Hilton) Hotel from the days when organizers went out on a limb to sell tickets for the unheard of price of $25 a plate.

Dignitaries from the leading Italian organizations join Father Lawrence Cozzi and Catholic Charities officials who came for the groundbreaking of Casa San Carlo, an independent-living apartment complex adjacent to Villa Scalabrini. This group was photographed in the 1980s.

Frank Catrambone (tailor and tuxedo rental proprietor) and friend entertained at the Villa Day celebration in the late 1970s.

Eleven
AMERICANIZATION

Over the past 100 years, Italians in Chicago have become Americanized. Whether it was taking out citizenship papers, service in the U.S. military, involvement in politics, choosing the United States over Italy in WW II, or succeeding at sports or entertainment careers, Italians gained acceptance and even respect from the dominant culture. Meanwhile, American society has moved away from its intolerant melting pot expectations to an acceptance of diversity. Many Chicago Italians today find it possible to be completely integrated in American society *and* to maintain Italian cultural practices.

John J. Petrone is among these boot camp recruits at the Great Lakes Naval Station in 1917. U.S. service in WW I offered many Italian immigrants a fast track to citizenship. Some Italian men returned to Italy to serve in the Old Country's military. (IAC 208.13.)

Bernardo Barasa

CANDIDATO REPUBBLICANO

A Giudice della Circuit Court

Elezione Giudiziarie Lunedì

6 Giugno 1921

Tutto ci fa arguire che il Cavaliere Barasa l'onorevole giudice della Corte Municipale otterrà una elezione plebiscitaria il prossi mo lunedì 6 giugno, quando avranno luog le elezioni dei giudici della Circuit Court di un giudice—presidente della Superio Court.

This clip from *La Tribuna Transatlantica* promotes Bernardo Barasa, Republican candidate for judge of the circuit court in the June 6, 1921 election. Though he was defeated soundly in a later primary bid for mayor of Chicago, Barasa came closer than any other Italian American to becoming mayor.

Under the watchful eye of the law, Judge Bernardo Barasa presides over the counting of the receipts for a fund-raiser on behalf of the victims of the Messina Earthquake in 1909. Italian and other immigrants have often dropped regional and class differences to come to the aid of homeland victims of disasters. (IAC 110.19.)

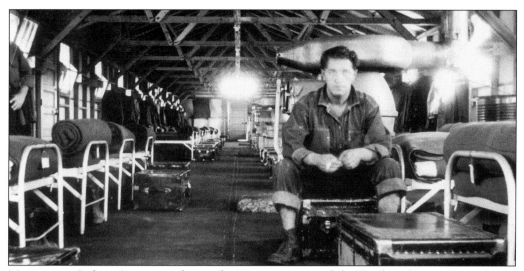

Many young Italian Americans during the Depression joined the Civilian Conservation Corps, where they were put to work for $30 per month with $25 of that going directly to their families.

This declaration of intent to become a citizen was also known as "first papers." Many researchers and genealogists have found these documents very useful in compiling data about Italian immigrants. In the Chicago Heights Public Library, there are over 3,000 such documents for European immigrants to that city.

The St. Anthony's *Broadcast* was a mimeograph publication that chronicled and exchanged information about scores of Roseland area servicemen stationed all over the globe during WW II. The staff, shown above, worked tirelessly to stretch their neighborhood network to include all the boys at the front. (IAC 55.27.)

Italian-American women in the Columbus Park Field House during WW II met under the auspices of the Red Cross to knit socks and other items for the soldiers. Such activities produced the needed items, and they involved the civilian populace more directly in the war effort. Thus, the war experience Americanized even the women on the homefront.

Il Duce is in Chicago! Shoe repairman Sam Vitale portrayed Benito Mussolini in a humorous Sunshine Club skit in 1933. Intergenerational and political conflicts over Mussolini troubled the Italian community in the late 1930s.

Italian Consul General and Chicago Heights Mayor Thomas address an outdoor group of Italian Americans in the 1920s. (IAC 52.1.)

This 1940s photograph captures a Chicago Heights gathering in an Italian neighborhood to honor the boys in the military and their families. WW II changed everything for Italians in Chicago.

Louis Panico, "King of the Wabash Blues," and his Orchestra pose for a publicity shot in 1938. Panico was one of the biggest success stories to come out of the Near West Side. He got his start in funeral bands and moved up to the Canton Tea Garden before making it big on the radio as one of the most popular musical groups in Chicago.

The semi-pro Melrose Park Panthers in the late 1930s included a number of Italian-American players. Then, as now, sports were an avenue to social acceptance into the mainstream—and they were fun. (IAC 190.2.)

Ron Santo, shown with his family at Wrigley Field, represents Italian-American achievement in sports that has enhanced their general acceptance in society. Harry Caray was another important Italian American on the local sports scene.

Twelve

PRESERVING THE

CULTURE

Historian Oscar Handlin has stressed that the migration process "uprooted" immigrants and robbed them of their culture. Since Columbus Day was made a national holiday (in large part, through the efforts of Chicago Congressman Frank Annunzio), it has become a focal point for the celebration of Italian-American culture. Enjoying less public notice than Columbus Day are the dozens of organizations like the Italian Cultural Center, Casa Italia, academic, folk, regional, educational, and artistic groups and individuals dedicating themselves, 100 years after migration, to the maintenance and promotion of Italian-American culture.

Cardinal Joseph Bernardin is shown here with children on Columbus Day. Having an Italian American as cardinal was a great source of pride for Italians in Chicago, and almost every large organization honored him with a testimonial dinner. This only heightened the anguish for Italians, when the archdiocese ordered a number of ethnic churches closed during the 1990s.

Columbus and Queen Isabella wave to Perennial Grand Marshall, Marco DiStefano along Dearborn Street in a 1980s Columbus Day Parade. Behind Columbus is the TV camera boom. The parade was a way for the Italian-American community to put its best foot forward both live and in the electronic media, sometimes nationwide on super station WGN-TV.

Spectators watch the Columbus Day Parade.

The Statue of Liberty passes Chicago's Picasso in the 1987 Columbus Day Parade.

It was standing room only at the Columbus Day mass at Our Lady of Pompeii Church in the early 1980s. The day's activities were permeated with a sense of community and a feeling of accomplishment and empowerment.

First Lady Pat Nixon and Mayor Richard J. Daley lead the Columbus Day Parade down State Street in the early 1970s. Pictured in the front lines are, from left to right, Gov. Dan Walker, Aldermen Vito Marzullo and Fred Roti, businessman Anthony Paterno, County Commissioner Frank Chesrow, and Parade Chair John Porcelli.

Marie Palello and others wave from their float in the Columbus Day Parade in 1981. The event includes over 100 units and, since it is held shortly before November elections, always draws more than its share of heavy-weight political figures.

This bronze statue by Moses Ezekiel is a momento of the 1893 Columbian Exposition. It once adorned the Columbus Memorial Building at State and Washington Streets and was saved by the Municipal Art League when the building was razed in 1959. The JCCIA raised funds to have it placed in the new Arrigo Park on the Near West Side in 1965.

Italian-American dignitaries came to the Columbus Day reception hosted by Mayor Harold Washington in the mid-1980s. Ethnic politics in Chicago accords attention to and respect for the full spectrum of ethnic groups on a regular basis. Italians take a back seat to no one in their desire to take full advantage of the process.

The Cusimano family pitches in to help the Chicago Public Library Cultural Center celebrate Christmas in 1981 by providing an authentic Italian Befana. Through the Joint Civic Committee of Italian Americans and the Italian Cultural Center, Italians have always been well-represented at city-wide, multicultural events.

Into the 1940s, an Italian language dramatic company led by Cristoforo and Fannie Da Sanza entertained audiences at the Washington School auditorium in Chicago Heights. The existence of such groups dispels the myth that Italian immigrants were totally uprooted from their culture and language.

Mom Lizzo baked bread for her family for over 40 years in a wood-burning oven. Italian immigrants, though lacking in formal education, came to the country with dozens of agricultural and homemaking skills that allowed them to cope and flourish as they "did for themselves" in the new American environment.

Batista Lizzo pours his homemade wine into gallon bottles. The mass marketing of Carlo Rossi and Gallo jug wines in the 1960s put a damper on many homemade wine operations. The California wines were consistently good, and the price was low enough to discourage even old-timers from going to the trouble, expense, and uncertainty of making their own wine.

Architectural model maker, Lucio Savoia, a native of Rome, shows off the 1:100 miniature of the Vatican, which he and his brother Atilio painstakingly created in the 1950s. His audience includes three of the greatest stars in the history of opera (Renata Tebaldi, Tito Gobbi, and Ilva Ligabue). In the 1980s, this exact replica was added to the permanent collection at the Italian Cultural Center, where it is a favorite attraction. This photograph was taken in 1965.

Francesco Ribaudo presents Seven Hills East owner Joseph Spavone with three murals of Rome landmarks in December 1971. Similar Ribaudo renditions of the Spanish Steps and Castel Sant'Angelo are on display at the Italian Cultural Center.

In the 1960s, the Scalabrini Fathers sponsored charter trips to Italy, anticipating a tourist boom that led thousands of first, second, and third generation Italian Americans to go "back" to Italy in search of their roots.

Fr. Pierini and Ardis Krainik join others in honoring Maestro Bruno Bartoletti, the musical director of the Lyric Opera for many years. The growing popularity of opera and the local and international role played by Italians has enhanced the image and self-image of Italian Americans.

Radio programmer Angelo Liberati is pictured here in December 1982. Of Roman origin, Liberati appealed to a younger, Italian-born audience. Among his many enterprises were stage shows featuring Italian super stars like Domenico Modugno and "Radio Uno," a 24-hour-a-day radio program direct from Italy.

In an era of ethnic revival, leaders of the Italian American Executives of Transportation and University of Illinois at Chicago students and faculty members gather to plan the Italians in Chicago Project in 1979.

For many years after WW II, Fr. Armando Pierini used his "L'Ora Cattolica" (Catholic Hour) to reach Italians on behalf of the Villa with a spiritual message and community information. He was greatly aided by his longtime assistant, Mary Mugnaini.

The Italian Cultural Center Singers and Dancers entertained countless festival audiences with their "Musical Journey Through Italy," which they performed under the leadership of Josephine LiPuma (standing center) from the 1970s into the 1990s. Their music perpetuated the culture for the older generations and introduced the traditional music of Italy to the younger generations of Italians.

An enthusiastic instructor conducts an Italian language class for young people. Italians in Chicago have not been especially successful at passing on the language to the third and fourth generations. Ethnic revivalists and the Italian government have continued to campaign for more (and better) language classes for children and adults.

Leaders of the Italian Cultural Center line up to cut the ribbon on the John Cadel gallery. They are, from left to right, Mario Spampinato (sculptor), Leonora LiPuma, John Bucci (designer and fabricator of the gallery), Consul General Teodoro Fuxa, Congressman Frank Annunzio, Fr. August Feccia (founder of the Center), Leonard Giampietro, and Fr. Peter Corbellini.